school - Schuel	2
travel - Reis	5
transport - Transport	8
city - Stadt	10
landscape - Landschaft	14
restaurant - Restaurant	17
supermarket - Läbensmittellade	20
drinks - Getränk	22
food - Läbensmittel	23
farm - Buurehof	27
house - Huus	31
living room - Stubä	33
kitchen - Chuchi	35
bathroom - Badzimmer	38
kids room - Chinderzimmer	42
clothing - Chleidig	44
office - Büro	49
economy - Wirtschaft	51
occupations - Brüef	53
tools - Werkzüüg	56
musical instruments - Musiginstrumänt	57
zoo - Zolli	59
sports - Sport	62
activities - Aktivitäte	63
family - Familiä	67
body - Körpär	68
hospital - Spital	72
emergency - Notfall	76
earth - Ärde	77
clock - Uhr	79
week - Wuche	80
year - Johr	81
shapes - Forme	83
colors - Farbä	84
opposites - Gägeteil	85
numbers - Zahlä	88
languages - Sprache	90
who / what / how - wär / was / wie	91
where - wo	92

Impressum
Verlag: BABADADA GmbH, Nedderfeld 112 , 22529 Hamburg
Geschäftsführer / Verlagsleitung: Harald Hof
Druck: Books on Demand GmbH, In de Tarpen 42, 22848 Norderstedt

Imprint
Publisher: BABADADA GmbH, Nedderfeld 112 , 22529 Hamburg, Germany
Managing Director / Publishing direction: Harald Hof
Print: Books on Demand GmbH, In de Tarpen 42, 22848 Norderstedt

school
Schuel

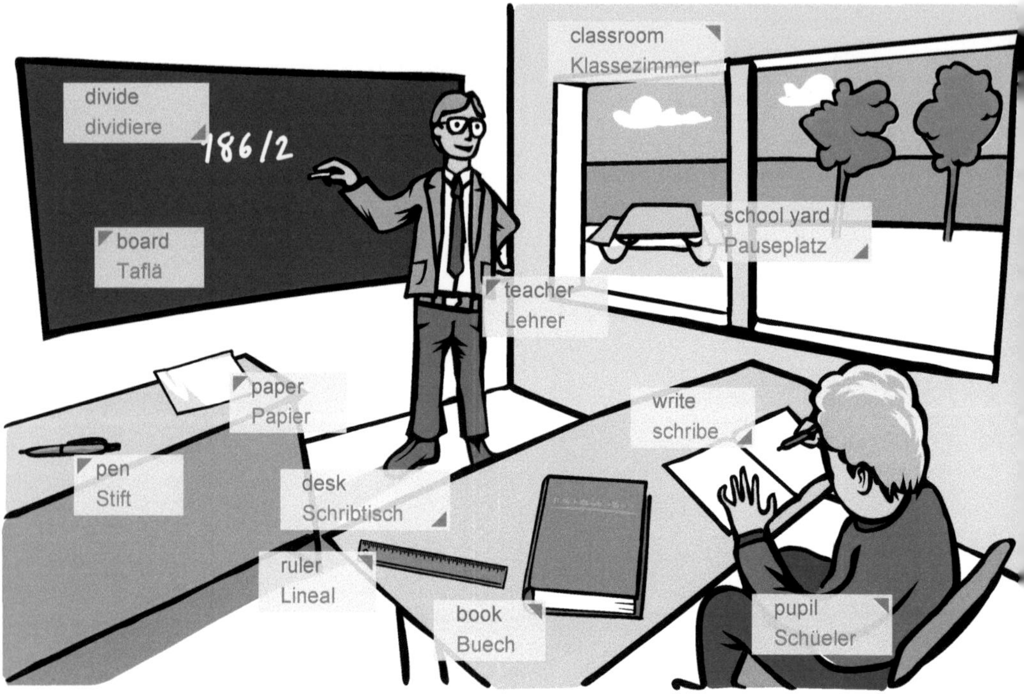

classroom
Klassezimmer
divide
dividiere
186/2
board
Taflä
school yard
Pauseplatz
teacher
Lehrer
paper
Papier
write
schribe
pen
Stift
desk
Schribtisch
ruler
Lineal
book
Buech
pupil
Schüeler

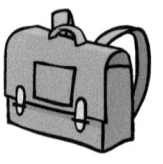

satchel
Thek

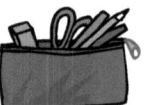

pencil case
Etui

pencil
Bleistift

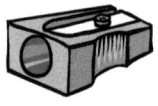

pencil sharpener
Spitzer

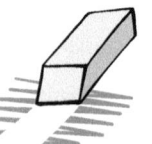

rubber
Radiergummi

drawing pad
Zeicheblock

drawing
Zeichnig

paintbrush
Pinsel

paint box
Malchaschte

scissors
Schär

glue
Liim

exercise book
Üebigsheft

homework
Huusufgabe

12

number
Zahl

2+2

add
addiere

5-2

subtract
subtrahiere

2×2

multiply
multipliziere

calculate
rächne

letter
Buechstabe

ABCDEFG HIJKLMN OPQRSTU VWXYZ

alphabet
Alphabet

word
Wort

text

Text

read

läse

chalk

Kriide

lesson

Lektion

register

Klassäbuech

examination

Prüefig

certificate

Zügnis

school uniform

Schueluniform

education

Usbildig

encyclopedia

Enzyklopädie

university

Universität

microscope

Mikroskop

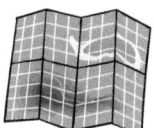

map

Charte

waste-paper basket

Papierchorb

travel
Reis

hotel
Hotel
Grand
hostel
Härbärg
ROOMS
EXCHANGE
currency exchange office
Wächselstube
car
Auto

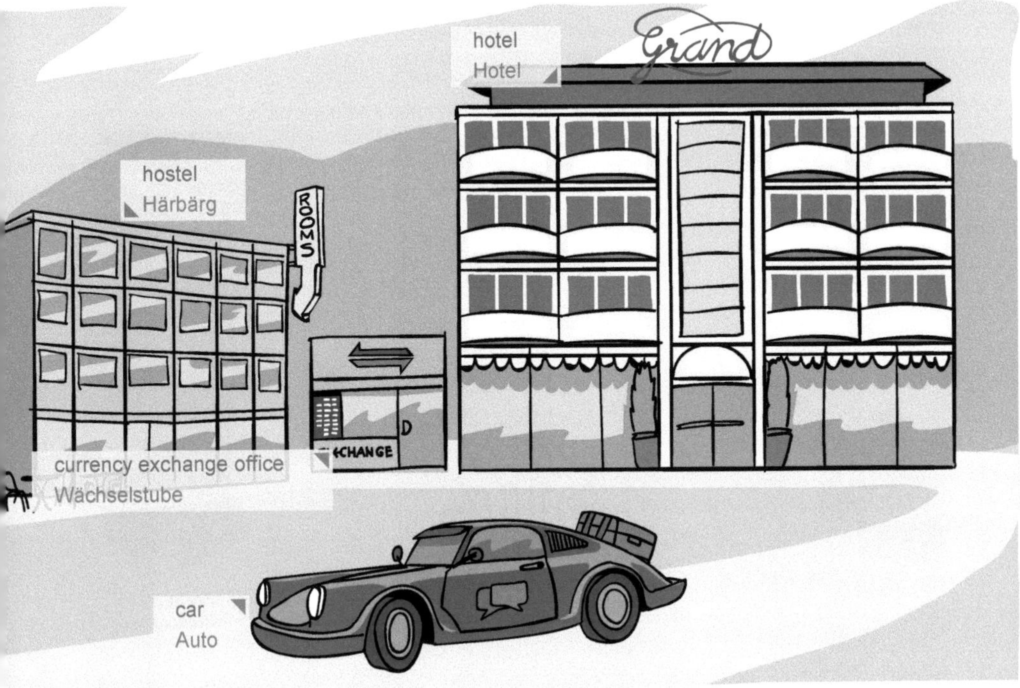

language

Sprach

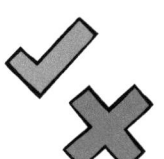

yes / no

jo / nei

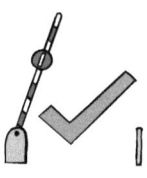

Okay

okay

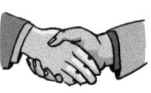

hello

Hallo

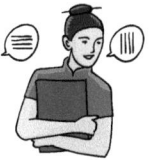

translator

Dolmetscher

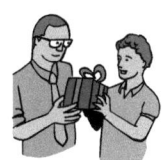

Thank you

Dankä

how much is...?

Was chostet...?

I don´t get it

Ich vrstahs nöd

problem

Problem

Good evening!

Guete Abig!

Good morning!

guete Morgä!

Good night!

guete Abig!

goodbye

Uf Wiederseh

direction

Richtig

luggage

Bagaasch

bag

Täsche

backpack

Rucksack

guest

Gast

room

Ruum

sleeping bag

Schlafsack

tent

Zält

tourist information

Touristeninformation

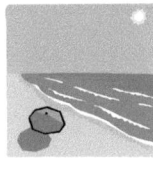

beach

Strand

credit card

Kreditkarte

breakfast

Zmorge

lunch

Zmittag

dinner

Znacht

Ticket

Billet

elevator

Ufzug

stamp

Briefmarke

border

Gränze

customs

Zoll

embassy

Botschaft

visa

Visum

passport

Pass

transport
Transport

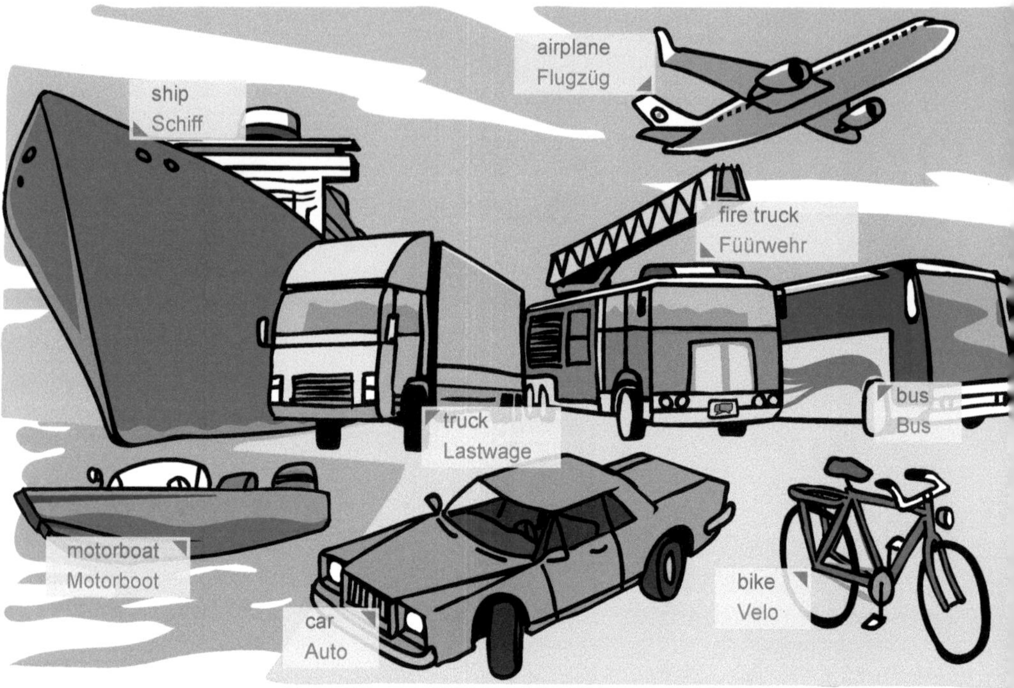

airplane
Flugzüg
ship
Schiff
fire truck
Füürwehr
truck
Lastwage
bus
Bus
motorboat
Motorboot
bike
Velo
car
Auto

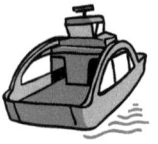

ferry
Fähri

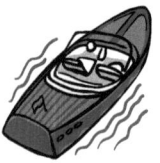

boat
Boot

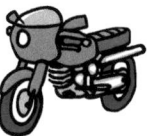

motorbike
Töff

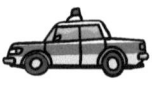

police car
Polizeiauto

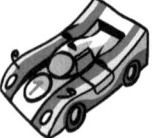

racing car
Rännauto

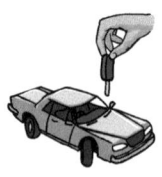

rental car
Mietwage

car sharing

Carsharing

tow truck

Abschleppwage

garbage truck

Chübelwage

engine

Motor

fuel

Benzin

fuel station

Tankstell

traffic sign

Verkehrsschild

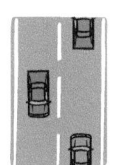

traffic

Verchehr

traffic jam

Stau

parking lot

Parkplatz

train station

Bahnhof

tracks

Schiene

train

Zug

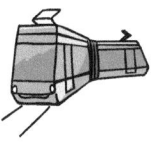

tram

Strassebahn

wagon

Wagon

helicopter

Helikopter

airport

Flughafe

tower

Tower

passenger

Passagier

container

Container

carton

Karton

cart

Chare

basket

Korb

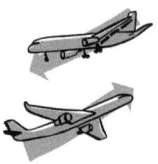

take off / land

starte / lande

city
Stadt

village

Dorf

city center

Stadtzentrum

house

Huus

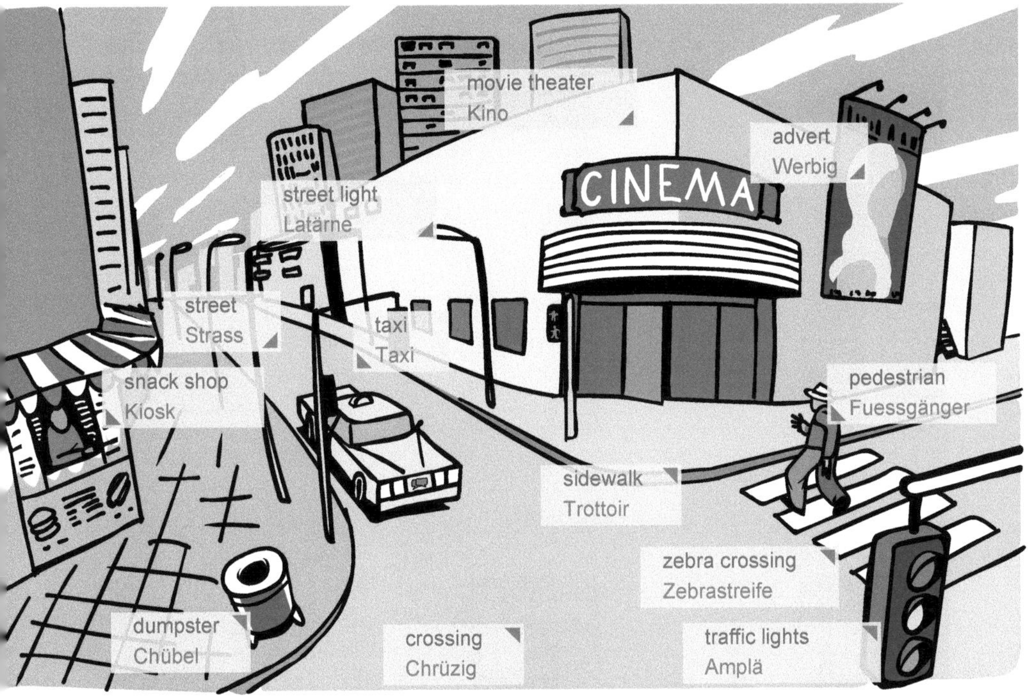

movie theater
Kino

advert
Werbig

street light
Latärne

CINEMA

street
Strass

taxi
Taxi

snack shop
Kiosk

pedestrian
Fuessgänger

sidewalk
Trottoir

zebra crossing
Zebrastreife

dumpster
Chübel

crossing
Chrüzig

traffic lights
Amplä

hut
Hütte

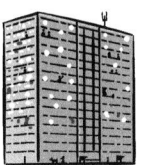

apartment
Wohnig

train station
Bahnhof

city hall
Gmeindshuus

museum
Museum

school
Schuel

university

Universität

bank

Bank

hospital

Spital

hotel

Hotel

pharmacy

Apotheke

office

Büro

book shop

Buechgschäft

shop

Gschäft

flower shop

Bluemelade

supermarket

Läbensmittellade

market

Märt

department store

Chaufhuus

fishmonger's shop

Fischhändler

mall

lihkaufszentrum

harbor

Hafe

park

Park

bench

Bank

bridge

Brugg

stairs

Stäge

subway

U-Bahn

tunnel

Tunnell

bus stop

Bushaltestell

bar

Bar

restaurant

Restaurant

postbox

Briefchastä

street sign

Strasseschild

parking meter

Parkuhr

zoo

Zolli

swimming pool

Badi

mosque

Moschee

farm

Buurehof

pollution

Umwältvrschmutzig

cemetery

Fridhof

church

Chile

playground

Spielplatz

temple

Tämpel

landscape
Landschaft

signpost
Wägwiiser

path
Wäg

meadow
Wise

stone
Stei

hiker
Wanderer

tree
Baum

river
Fluss

grass
Gras

flower
Bluamä

valley

Tal

hill

Bärg

lake

See

forest

Wald

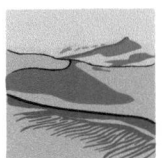

desert

Wüeschti

volcano

Vulkan

castle

Schloss

rainbow

Rägeboge

mushroom

Pilz

palm tree

Palme

mosquito

Moskito

fly

Fliege

ant

Ameise

bee

Biendli

spider

Spinne

landscape - Landschaft

beetle

Chäfer

frog

Frosch

squirrel

Eichhörnli

hedgehog

Igel

hare

Haas

owl

Üle

bird

Vogu

swan

Schwan

boar

Wildschwein

deer

Hirsch

moose

Elch

dam

Damm

wind turbine

Windturbine

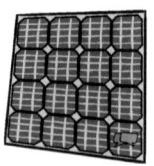

solar panel

Sunnekollektor

climate

Klima

waiter
Chällner

menu
Spiischartä

chair
Stuehl

soup
Suppä

pizza
Pizza

cutlery
Bsteck

tablecloth
Tischdecki

starter
Vorspiies

main course
Hauptgricht

dessert
Dessert

drinks
Getränk

food
Läbensmittel

bottle
Fläsche

fast food

Fast Food

street food

Street Food

teapot

Teechanne

sugar bowl

Zuckerdosä

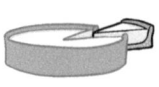

portion

Portion

espresso machine

Espressomaschine

high chair

Hochstuehl

bill

Rächnig

tray

Tablett

knife

Mässer

fork

Gable

spoon

Löffel

teaspoon

Teelöffel

serviette

Serviette

glass

Glas

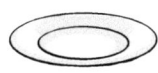

plate

Täller

soup plate

Suppetällär

saucer

Untertasse

sauce

Sose

salt shaker

Salzstreuer

pepper mill

Pfäffermühli

vinegar

Essig

oil

Öl

spices

Gwürz

ketchup

Ketchup

mustard

Sänf

mayonnaise

Mayonnaise

supermarket
Läbensmittellade

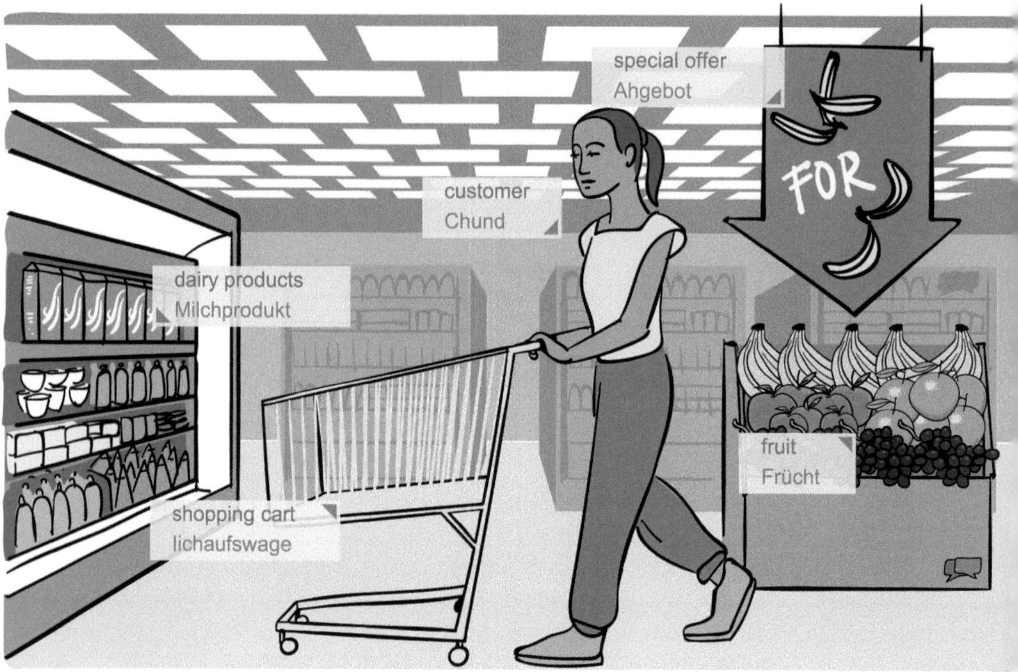

special offer
Ahgebot
FOR
customer
Chund
dairy products
Milchprodukt
shopping cart
lichaufswage
fruit
Frücht

BUTCHERS

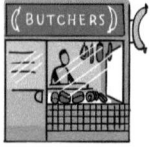

butcher's shop

Schlachter

BAKERY

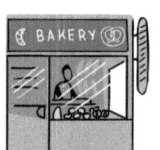

bakery

Beck

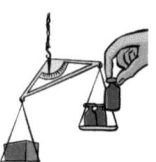

weigh

wiege

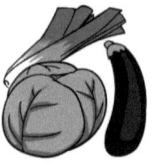

vegetables

Gmües

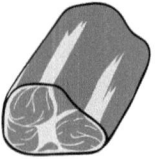

meat

Fleisch

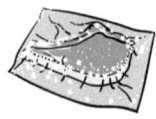

frozen food

Tiefkühlprodukt

cold cuts

Ufschnitt

canned food

die Konsärve

detergent

Wöschmittel

candy

Süessigkeite

household products

Huushaltartikel

cleaning products

Putzmittel

sales representative

Verchäuferin

cash register

Kassä

cashier

Kassierer

shopping list

Ihchaufsliste

opening hours

Öffnigszite

wallet

das Portemonnaie

credit card

Kreditkarte

bag

Täsche

plastic bag

Plastiksack

water
······
Wasser

juice
······
Saft

milk
······
Milch

coke
······
Cola

wine
······
Wii

beer
······
Bier

alcohol
······
Alkohol

cocoa
······
Ovi

tea
······
Tee

coffee
······
Kafi

espresso
······
Espresso

cappuccino
······
Cappuccino

banana

Banane

apple

Öpfel

orange

Orange

melon

Melone

lemon

Zitrone

carrot

Rüebli

garlic

Chnoobli

bamboo

Bambus

onion

Zwiblä

mushroom

Pilz

nuts

Nüss

noodles

Nudle

spaghetti

Spaghetti

rice

Riis

salad

Salat

fries

Pommfrit

fried potatoes

Bratherdöpfel

pizza

Pizza

hamburger

Hamburgär

sandwich

Sandwich

escalope

Gotlett

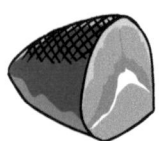

ham

Schinkä

salami

Salami

sausage

Würschtli

chicken

Huehn

roast

Bratä

fish

Fisch

porridge oats

Haferflocke

muesli

Müesli

cornflakes

Cornflakes

flour

Mähl

croissant

Gipfeli

bread roll

Brötli

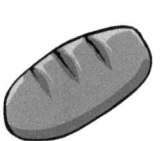

bread

Brot

toast

Toscht

cookies

Guetzli

butter

Butter

curd

Quark

cake

Chueche

egg

Ei

fried egg

Spiegelei

cheese

Chäs

ice cream

Glace

sugar

Zucker

honey

Honig

jelly

Gonfi

nougat cream

Nougat-Creme

curry

Curry

farm
Buurehof

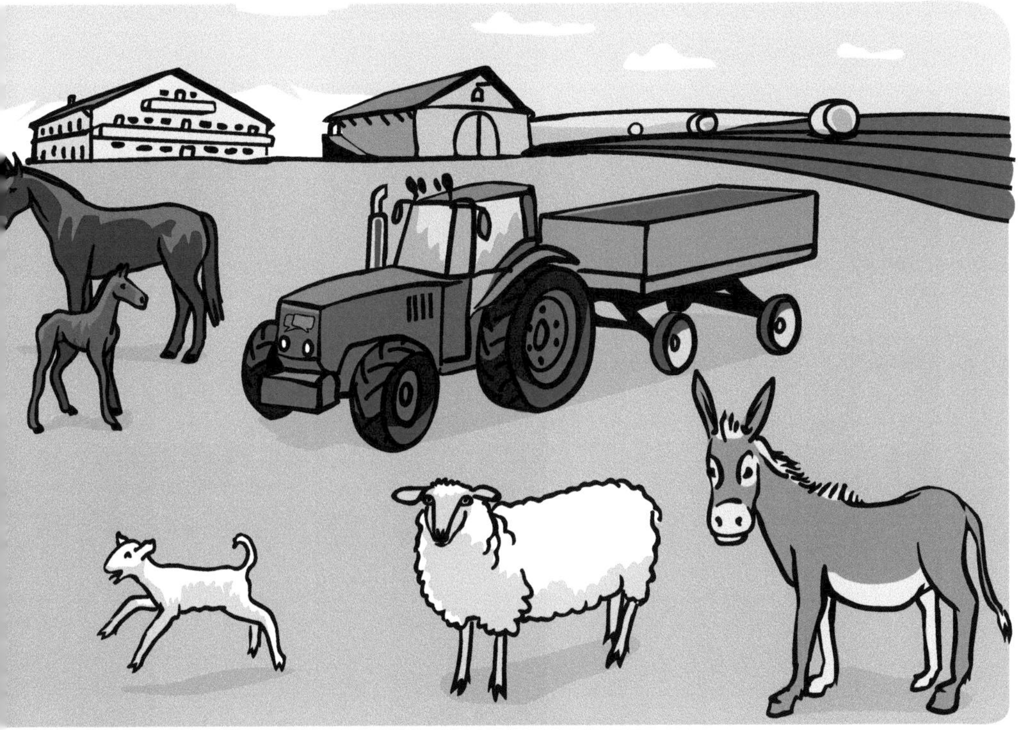

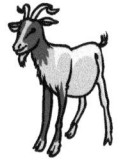

goat

Geiss

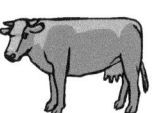

cow

Chueh

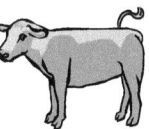

calf

Chalb

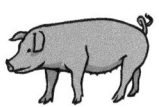

pig

Sau

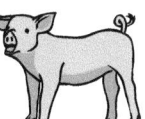

piglet

Ferkel

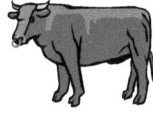

bull

Rind

goose
Gans

duck
Änte

chick
Küke

hen
Huähn

cockerel
Güggel

rat
Ratte

cat
Chatz

mouse
Muus

ox
Ochse

dog
Hund

dog house
Hundehütte

garden hose
Garteschluuch

watering can
Giesschanne

scythe
Sägese

plow
Pflueg

sickle

Sichel

hoe

Hacke

pitchfork

Heugable

axe

Axt

pushcart

Garette

trough

Trog

milk can

Milchchanne

sack

Sack

fence

Haag

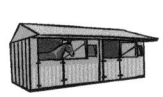

stable

Gadä

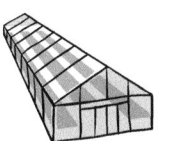

greenhouse

Gwächshuus

soil

Bode

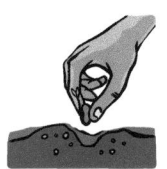

seed

Soome

fertilizer

Dünger

combine harvester

Mähdrescher

harvest

ärnte

harvest

Ärnte

yams

Yamswurzle

wheat

Weize

soya

Soja

potato

Härdöpfel

corn

Mais

rapeseed

Raps

fruit tree

Obstbaum

manioc

Maniok

grain

Getreide

living room

Stubä

bathroom

Badzimmer

kitchen

Chuchi

bedroom

Schlofzimmer

kids room

Chinderzimmer

dining room

Ässzimmer

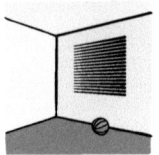

floor
Bodä

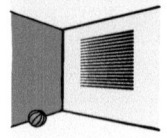

wall
Wand

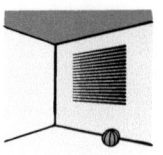

ceiling
Decki

cellar
Chäller

sauna
Sauna

balcony
Balkon

terrace
Terasse

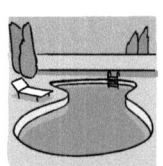

pool
Pool

lawn mower
Rasemäier

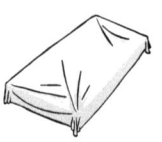

sheet
Bettbezug

bedspread
Bettdecki

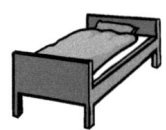

bed
Bett

broom
Bäse

bucket
Chübel

switch
Schalter

living room
Stubä

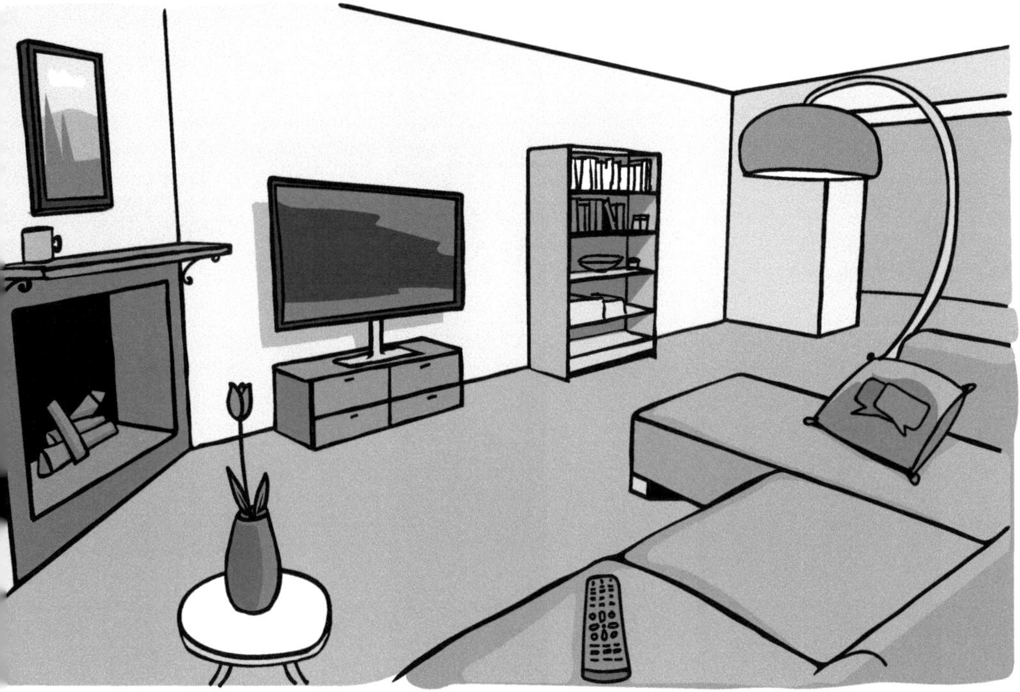

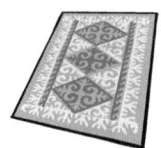

carpet
Teppich

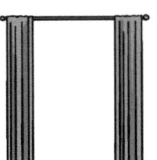

drape
Vorhang

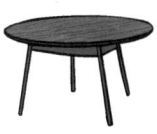

table
Tisch

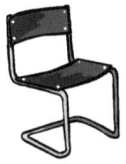

chair
Stuehl

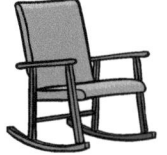

rocking chair
Schaukelstuehl

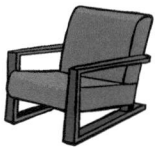

armchair
Sässel

book
Buech

blanket
Decki

decoration
Dekoration

firewood
Füürholz

film
Film

stereo system
Stereoahlag

key
Schlüssel

newspaper
Ziitig

painting
Bild

poster
Poster

radio
Radio

notebook
Notizblock

vacuum cleaner
Staubsuuger

cactus
Kaktus

candle
Chärze

kitchen
Chuchi

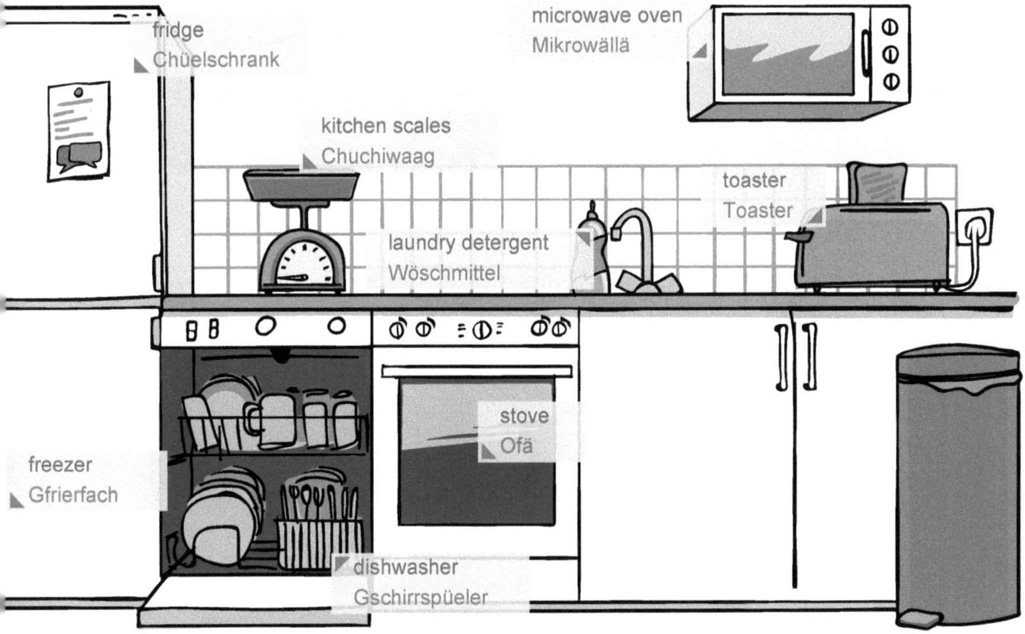

fridge
Chüelschrank
microwave oven
Mikrowällä
kitchen scales
Chuchiwaag
toaster
Toaster
laundry detergent
Wöschmittel
stove
Ofä
freezer
Gfrierfach
dishwasher
Gschirrspüeler

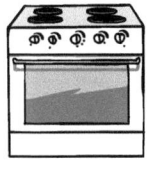

cooker
Härd

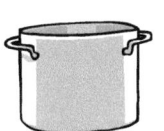

pot
Topf

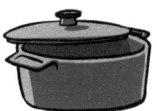

cast-iron pot
Iisetopf

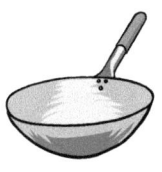

wok / kadai
Wok / Kadai

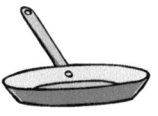

pan
Pfanne

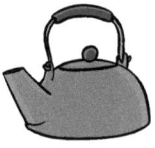

kettle
Wasserchocher

steamer

Dampfer

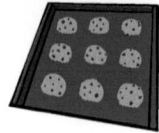

baking tray

Bachbläch

crockery

Gschirr

mug

Bächer

bowl

Schale

chopsticks

Stäbli

ladle

Suppechellä

spatula

Pfannewänder

whisk

Schneebäse

strainer

Sieb

sieve

Sieb

grater

Raffle

mortar

Mörser

barbecue

Grill

fireplace

Füürstell

chopping board
Schniidbrätt

rolling pin
Nudelholz

corkscrew
Korkäzieher

can
Dosä

can opener
Dosäöffner

oven cloth
Topflappä

sink
Wöschbecki

brush
Bürste

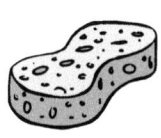

sponge
Schwumm

blender
Mixer

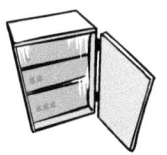

deep freezer
Gfrierschrank

baby bottle
Babyfläschli

tap
Hahnä

bathroom
Badzimmer

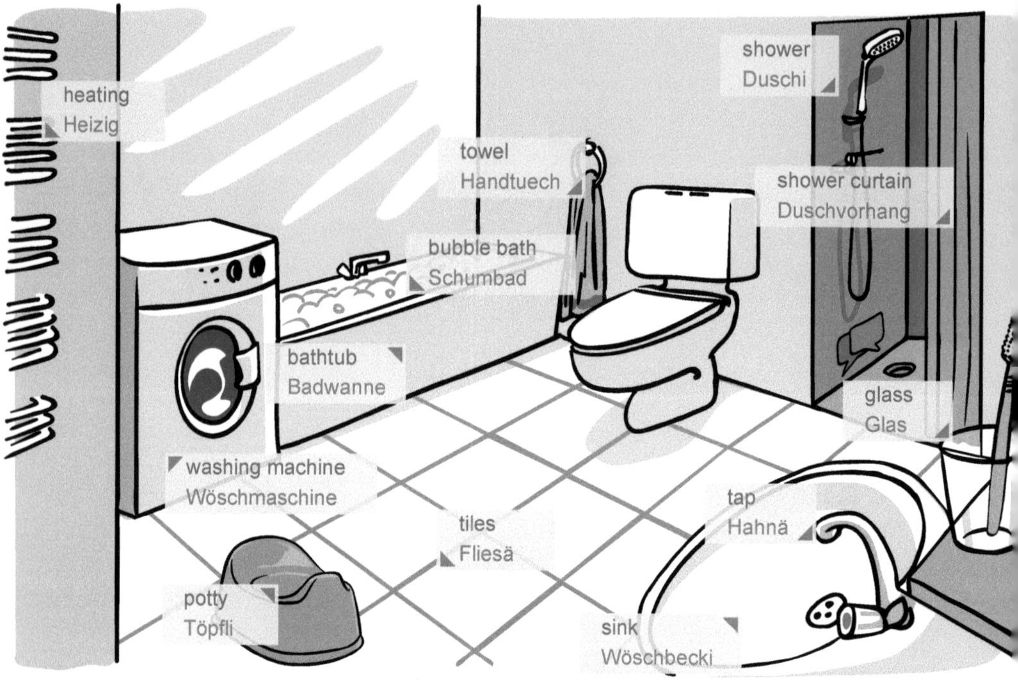
heating
Heizig
towel
Handtuech
shower
Duschi
shower curtain
Duschvorhang
bubble bath
Schumbad
bathtub
Badwanne
glass
Glas
washing machine
Wöschmaschine
tap
Hahnä
tiles
Fliesä
potty
Töpfli
sink
Wöschbecki

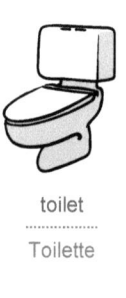

toilet

Toilette

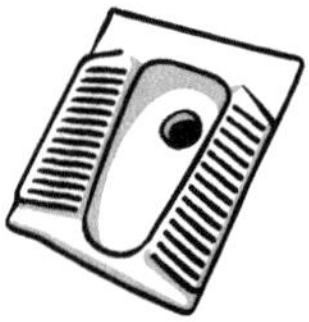

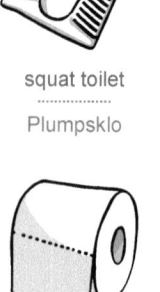

squat toilet

Plumpsklo

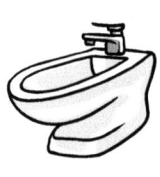

bidet

Bidet

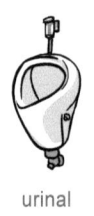

urinal

Pissoir

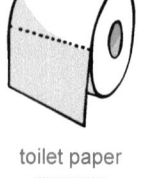

toilet paper

Toilettepapier

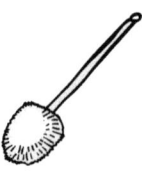

toilet brush

Toilettebürschteli

toothbrush

Zahbürstä

toothpaste

Zahpasta

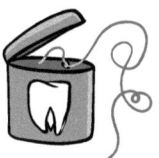

dental floss

Zahnsiide

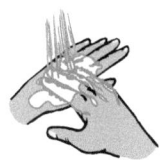

wash

wäsche

hand shower

Handduschi

douche

Intiimduschi

basin

Wöschbecki

back brush

Ruggäbürste

soap

Seifä

shower gel

Duschgel

shampoo

Shampoo

flannel

Waschlappä

drain

Abfluss

creme

Creme

deodorant

Deo

mirror

Spiegel

hand mirror

Handspiegel

razor

Rasierer

shaving foam

Rasierschuum

aftershave

Aftershave

comb

Schträäl

brush

Bürstä

hair-dryer

Föhn

hairspray

Hoorspray

makeup

Makeup

lipstick

Lippestift

nail varnish

Nagellack

cotton wool

Wattä

nail scissors

Nagelscher

perfume

Parfum

washbag

Necessaire

stool

Schemel

weighing scales

Waag

bathrobe

Badmantel

rubber gloves

Gummihändscheh

tampon

Tampon

sanitary towel

Damebinde

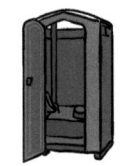

chemical toilet

chemischi Toilette

kids room

Chinderzimmer

alarm clock
Wecker
cuddly toy
Kuscheltier
toy car
Spielzügauto
rattle
Rassle
doll's house
Puppehuus
present
Gschänk

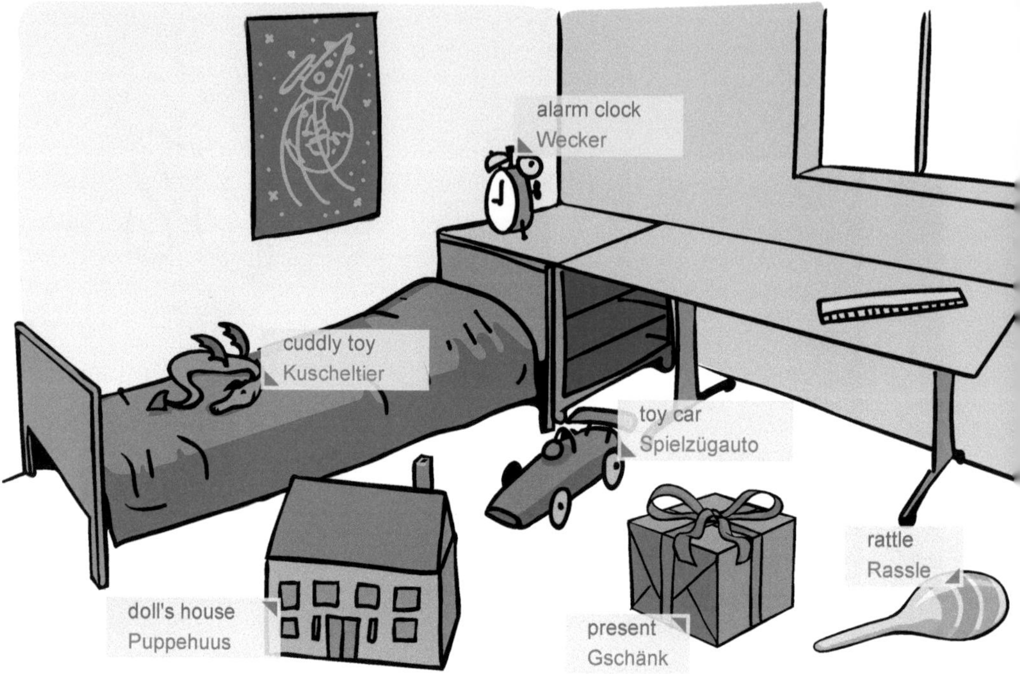

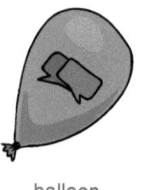

balloon

Ballon

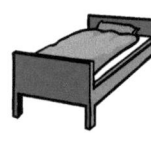

bed

Bett

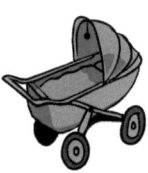

stroller

Chinderwage

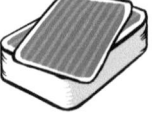

deck of cards

Chartespiel

jigsaw

Puzzle

SUPER MEGA

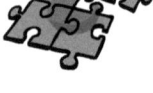

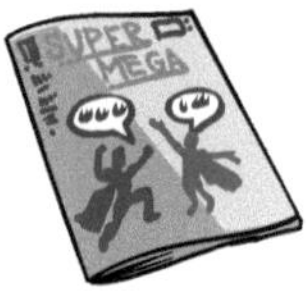

comic

Comic

lego bricks

Legos

toy blocks

Baustei

action figure

Action Figur

romper suit

Strampli

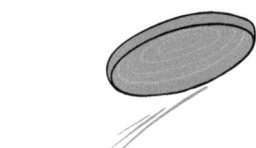

frisbee

Frisbee

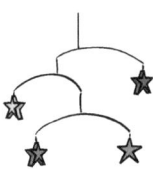

mobile

Mobile

board game

Brättspiel

dice

Würfäl

model train set

Modellisebahn

pacifier

Nuggi

party

Party

picture book

Bilderbuch

ball

Ball

doll

Puppä

play

spiele

sandpit

Sandchaschte

swing

Gigampfi

toys

Spielzüg

video game console

Videospielkonsole

tricycle

Dreirad

teddy bear

Teddy

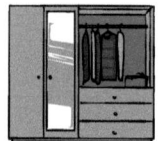

wardrobe

Chleiderschrank

clothing
Chleidig

socks

Sockä

stockings

Strümpf

tights

Strumpfhosä

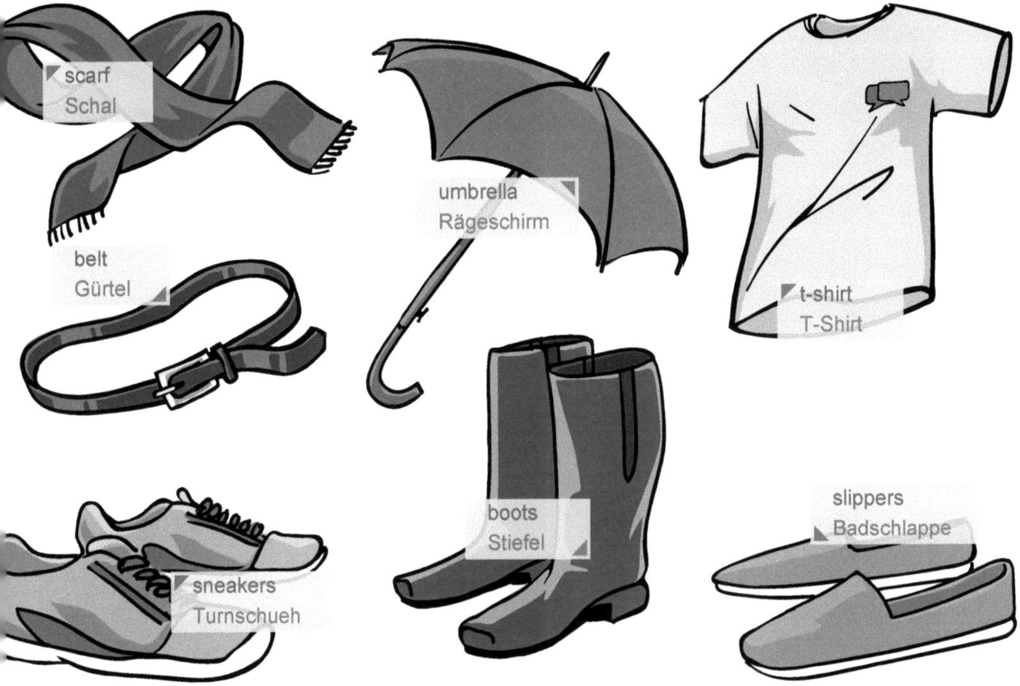

scarf
Schal

belt
Gürtel

umbrella
Rägeschirm

t-shirt
T-Shirt

boots
Stiefel

slippers
Badschlappe

sneakers
Turnschueh

sandals
Sandalä

shoes
Schueh

rubber boots
Gummistiefel

underwear
Untrhosä

bra
BH

undershirt
Underlibli

body
Body

pants
Hosä

jeans
Jeans

skirt
Rock

blouse
Bluse

shirt
Hömli

pullover
Pulli

sweater
Kapuzepulli

blazer
Blazer

jacket
Jacke

coat
Mantel

raincoat
Rägämantel

costume
Chostüm

dress
Chleid

wedding dress
Hochziitskleid

suit

Ahzug

nightgown

Nachthömli

pajamas

Pyjama

sari

Sari

headscarf

Chopftuäch

turban

Turban

burka

Burka

kaftan

Kaftan

abaya

Abaya

swimsuit

Badchleid

trunks

Badhose

shorts

churzi Hosä

tracksuit

Trainer

apron

Schürze

gloves

Händsche

button

Chnopf

glasses

Brüllä

bracelet

Armband

necklace

Chetti

ring

Ring

earring

Ohrering

cap

Chappe

coat hanger

Chleiderbügel

hat

Huet

tie

Grawattä

zip

Riissverschluss

helmet

Helm

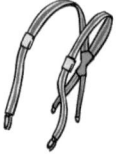

braces

Hosäträger

school uniform

Schueluniform

uniform

Uniform

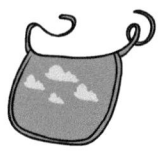

bib

Lätzli

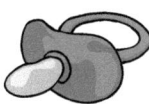

pacifier

Nuggi

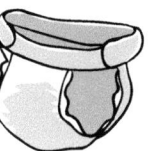

diaper

Windle

office
Büro

server
Server
filing cabinet
Akteschrank
printer
Drucker
paper
Papier
monitor
Monitor
mouse
Muus
desk
Schribtisch
folder
Ordner
keyboard
Taschtatur
chair
Stuehl
waste-paper basket
Papierchorb
computer
Computer

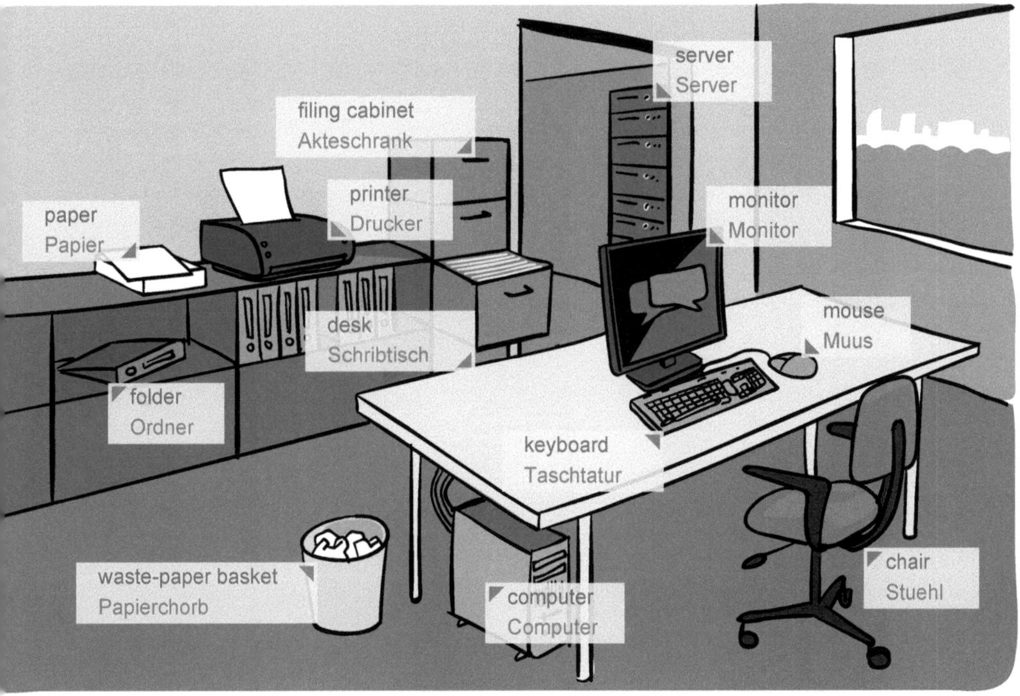

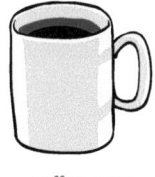

coffee mug

Kafibächer

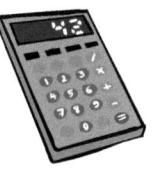

calculator

Tascherächner

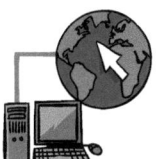

internet

Internet

laptop

Laptop

letter

Brief

message

Nochricht

cell phone

Mobiltelefon

network

Netzwärk

photocopier

Kopierer

software

Software

telephone

Telefon

plug socket

Steckdosä

fax machine

Fax

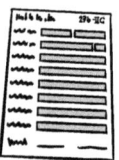

form

Formular

document

Dokumänt

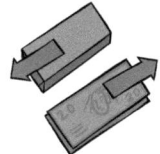

buy

chaufe

pay

zahle

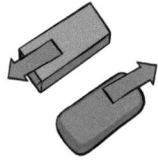

trade

handle

money

Gäld

USD

dollar

Dollar

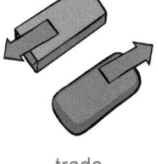

EUR

euro

Euro

JPY

yen

Yen

RUB

rouble

Rubel

CHF

Swiss franc

Frankä

CNY

renminbi yuan

Renminbi Yuan

INR

rupee

Rupie

cash point

Gäldautomat

currency exchange office

Wächselstube

gold

Gold

silver

Silber

oil

Öl

energy

Energie

price

Priis

contract

Vertrag

tax

Stüür

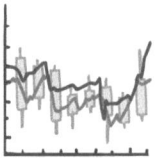

stock

Aktie

work

schaffe

employee

Mitarbeiter

employer

Arbeitgeber

factory

Fabrik

shop

Gschäft

police officer
Polizischt

fireman
Füürwehrmaa

pilot
Pilot

cook
Choch

doctor
Arzt

gardener
Gärtner

carpenter
Zimmermah

seamstress
Näheri

judge
Richter

chemist
Chemiker

actor
Darsteller

bus driver

Busfahrer

taxi driver

Taxifahrer

fisherman

Fischer

cleaning lady

Putzfrau

roofer

Dachdecker

waiter

Chällner

hunter

Jäger

painter

Moler

baker

Bäcker

electrician

Elektriker

builder

Bauarbeiter

engineer

Ingenieur

butcher

Schlachter

plumber

Klämpner

postman

Pöschtler

soldier

Soldat

architect

Architekt

cashier

Kassierer

florist

Florischt

hairdresser

Frisör

conductor

Kontrolleur

mechanic

Mechaniker

captain

Kapitän

dentist

Zahnarzt

scientist

Wüsseschaftler

rabbi

Rabbi

imam

Imam

monk

Mönch

pastor

Pfarrer

tools
Werkzüüg

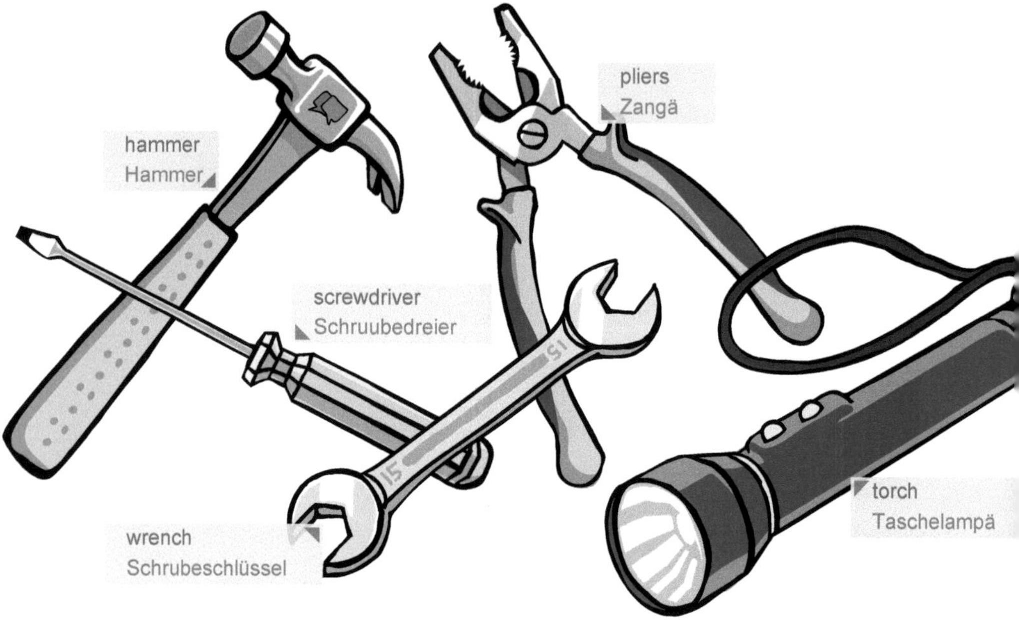
pliers
Zangä
hammer
Hammer
screwdriver
Schruubedreier
torch
Taschelampä
wrench
Schrubeschlüssel

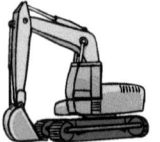

excavator
Bagger

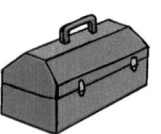

toolbox
Werkzüügchaschte

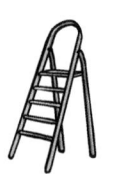

ladder
Leitere

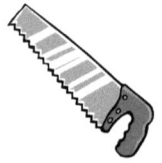

saw
Sagi

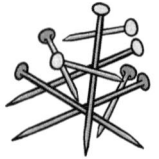

nails
Negel

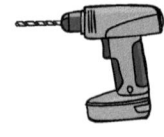

drill
Bohrer

repair

flicke

shovel

Schufle

Damn!

Mischt!

dustpan

Ascheschufle

paint can

Farbchübel

screws

Schruube

musical instruments
Musiginstrumänt

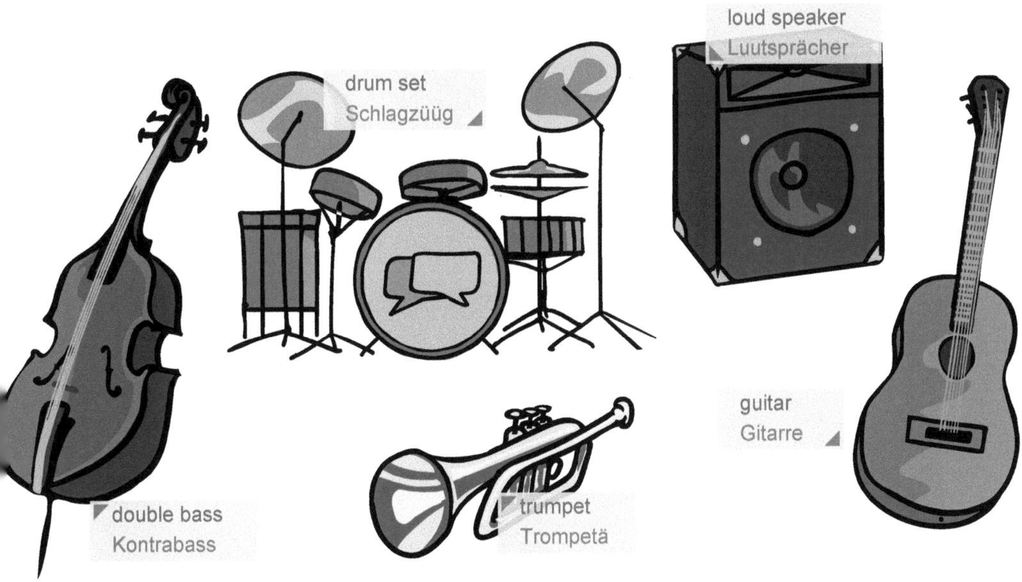

drum set
Schlagzüüg

loud speaker
Luutsprächer

guitar
Gitarre

double bass
Kontrabass

trumpet
Trompetä

piano

Klavier

violin

Violine

bass

Bass

timpani

Pauke

drums

Trummle

keyboard

Keyboard

saxophone

Saxophon

flute

Flöte

microphone

Mikrofon

ZOO
Zolli

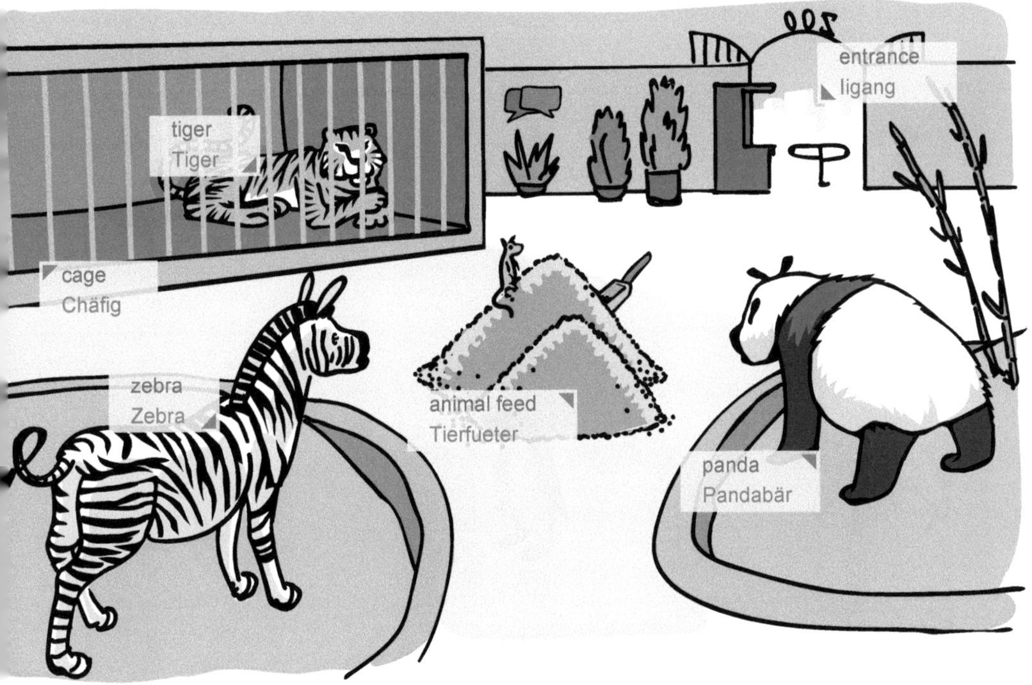
entrance
Iigang
tiger
Tiger
cage
Chäfig
zebra
Zebra
animal feed
Tierfueter
panda
Pandabär

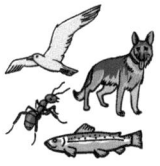

animals

Tier

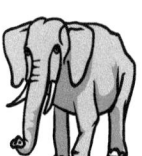

elephant

Elefant

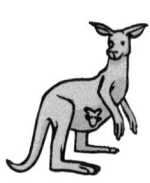

kangaroo

Känguru

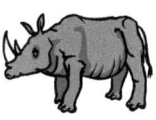

rhino

Nashorn

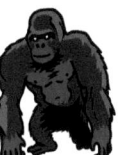

gorilla

Gorilla

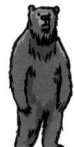

bear

Bär

camel

Kamel

ostrich

Struss

lion

Leu

monkey

Aff

flamingo

Flamingo

parrot

Papagei

polar bear

Iisbär

penguin

Pinguin

shark

Hai

peacock

Pfau

snake

Schlangä

crocodile

Krokodil

zookeeper

Zoowärter

seal

Robbä

jaguar

Jaguar

pony
Pony

leopard
Leopard

hippo
Nilpfärd

giraffe
Giraff

eagle
Adler

boar
Wildschwein

fish
Fisch

turtle
Schildkrot

walrus
Walross

fox
Fuchs

gazelle
Gazelle

American football
American Football

cycling
Velofahre

tennis
Tennis

basketball
Basketball

swimming
Schwümmä

boxing
Boxä

ice hockey
Iishockey

soccer	badminton	athletics
Fuessball	Badminton	Liechtathletik

handball	skiing	polo
Handball	Skifahre	Polo

activities
Aktivitäte

jump
springä
hug
umarme
laugh
lachä
walk
gah
sing
singe
dream
troime
pray
bätte
kiss
küssä

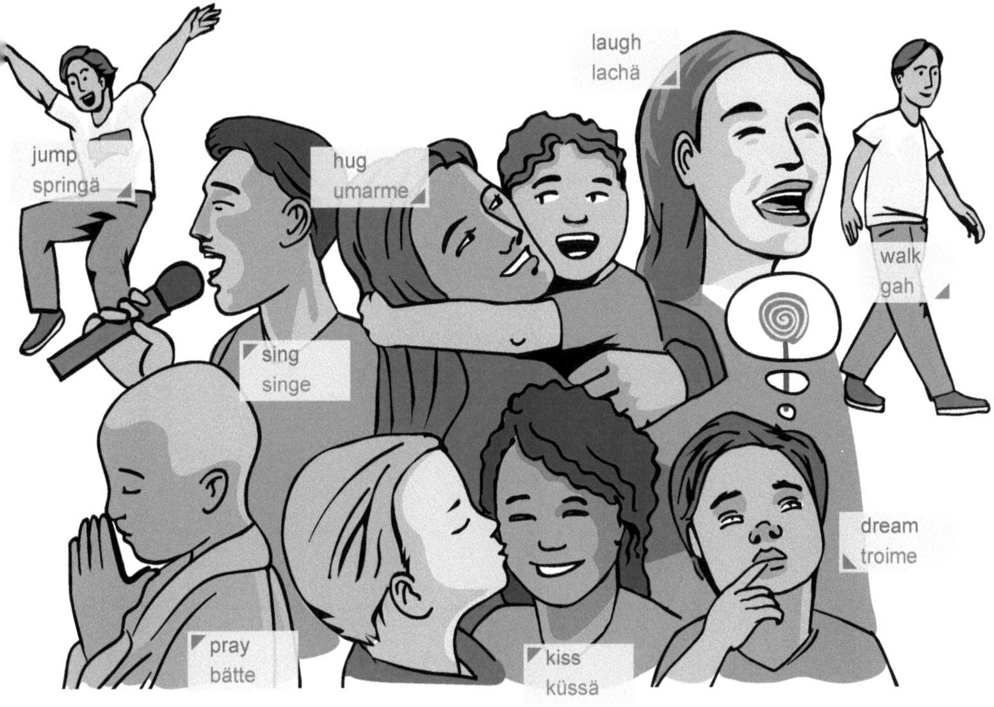

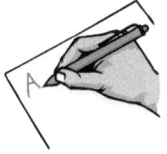

write

schribe

draw

zeichne

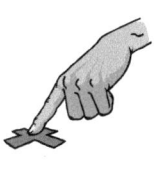

show

zeige

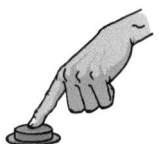

push

schiebe

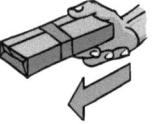

give

gäh

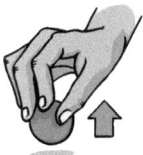

take

näh

have

händ

do

mache

be

sy

stand

stah

run

laufe

pull

zieh

throw

rüerä

fall

fallä

lie

ligge

wait

warte

carry

träge

sit

sitze

get dressed

ahzieh

sleep

schlafe

wake up

ufwache

look at

ahluege

cry

brüele

stroke

striichle

comb

bürste

talk

redä

understand

verschtah

ask

froog

listen

lose

drink

trinke

eat

ässe

tidy up

ufruume

love

liebe

cook

chochä

drive

fahre

fly

flüge

activities - Aktivitäte

sail
segle

calculate
rächne

read
läse

learn
leerä

work
schaffe

marry
hürate

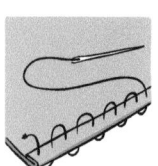

sew
näije

brush teeth
Zäh putze

kill
töte

smoke
schlootä

send
sände

activities - Aktivitäte

family
Familiä

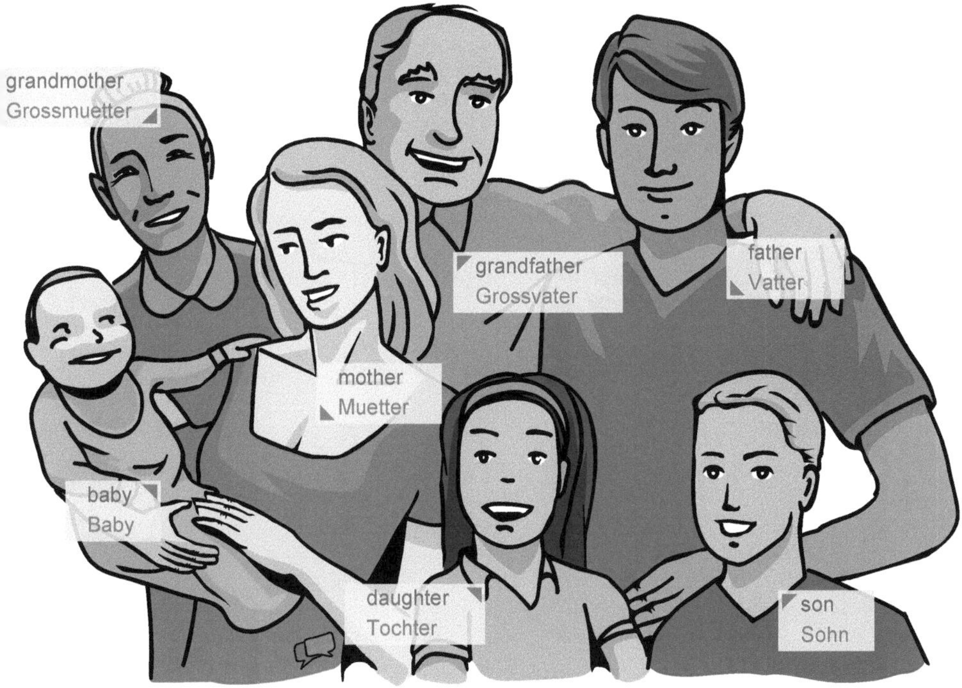
grandmother
Grossmuetter
grandfather
Grossvater
father
Vatter
mother
Muetter
baby
Baby
daughter
Tochter
son
Sohn

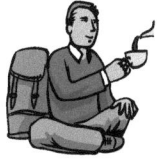

guest
Gast

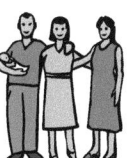

aunt
Tante

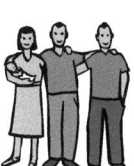

uncle
Unkel

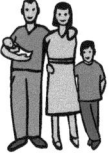

brother
Brüeder

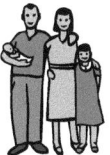

sister
Schwöschter

body
Körpär

forehead
Stirn
eye
Aug
shoulder
Schultere
finger
Fingär
face
Gsicht
chin
Chüni
hand
Hand
leg
Bei
breast
Bruscht
arm
Arm

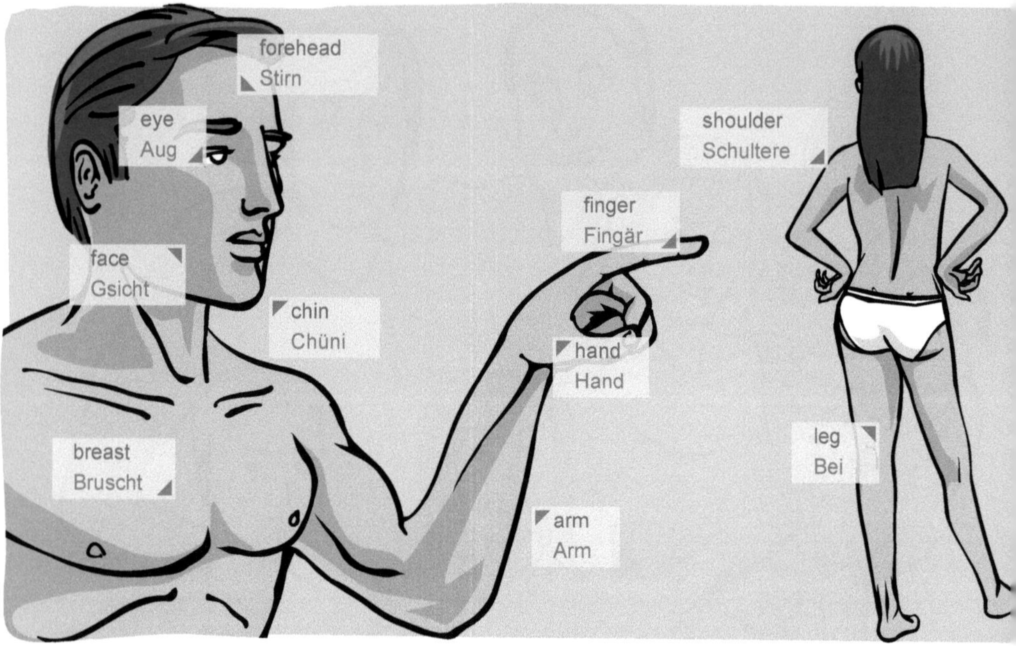

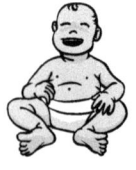

baby
Baby

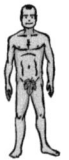

man
Mah

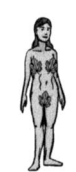

woman
Frau

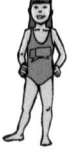

girl
Meitli

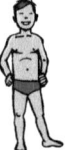

boy
Bueb

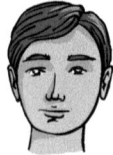

head
Chopf

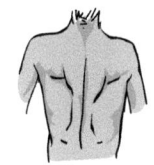	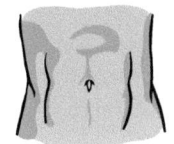	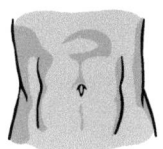
back	belly	navel
Ruggä	Buuch	Buchnabel
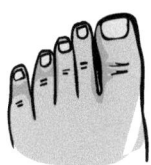	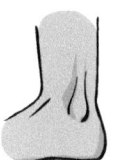	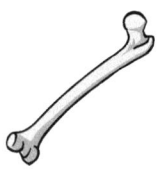
toe	heel	bone
Zäche	Fersä	Knoche
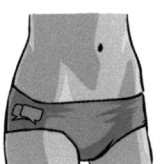	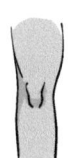	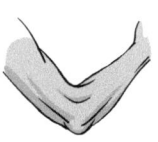
hip	knee	elbow
Hüfte	Chnü	Ellbogä
	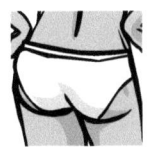	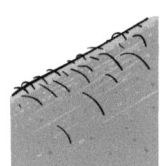
nose	buttocks	skin
Nase	Füdli	Hut
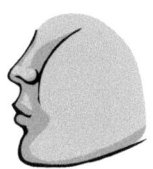	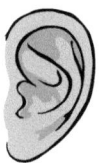	
cheek	ear	lip
Bagge	Ohr	Lippe

	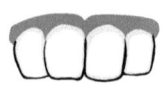	
mouth	tooth	tongue
Muul	Zah	Zungä
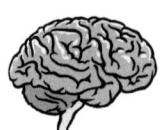	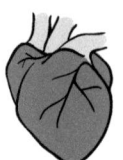	
brain	heart	muscle
Hirni	Härz	Muskel
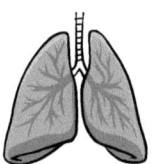		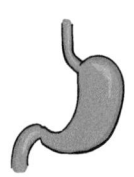
lung	liver	stomach
Lungä	Läberä	Magen
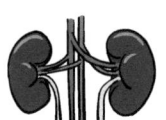		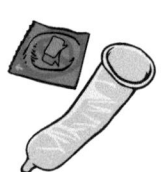
kidneys	sex	condom
Nierä	Gschlächtsvrkehr	Kondom
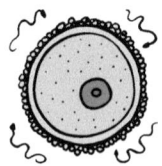		
ovum	semen	pregnancy
Eizälle	Soome	Schwangerschaft

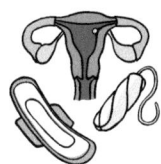

menstruation

Menstruation

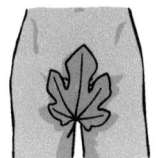

vagina

Vagina

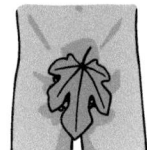

penis

Penis

eyebrow

Augebrauä

hair

Haar

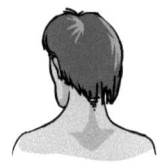

neck

Hals

body - Körpär
71

hospital
Spital

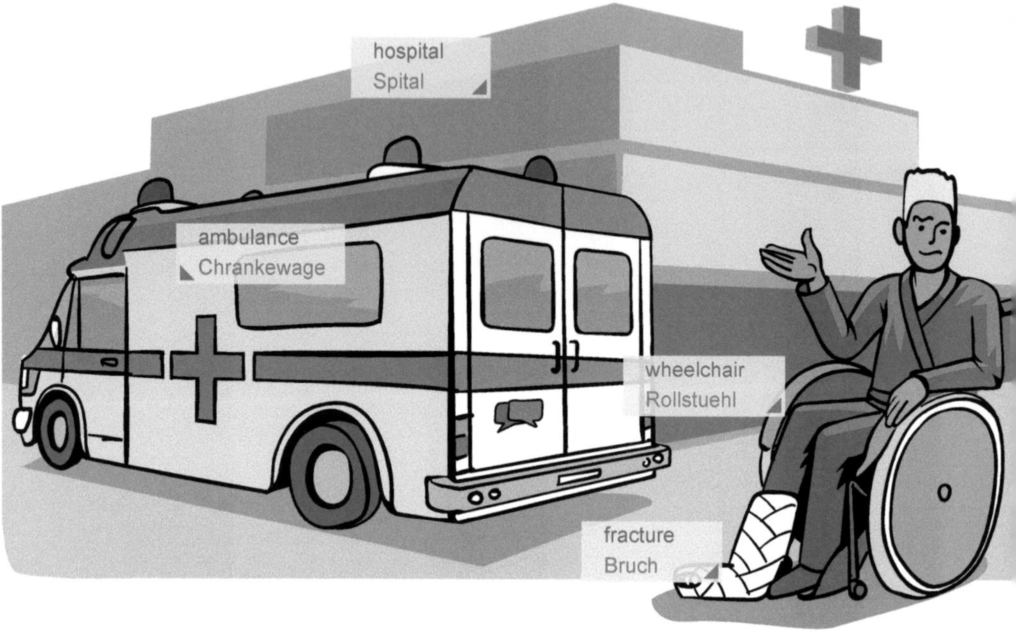

hospital
Spital
ambulance
Chrankewage
wheelchair
Rollstuehl
fracture
Bruch

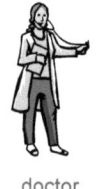

doctor

Arzt

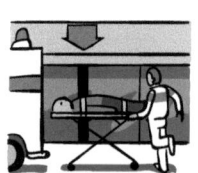

emergency room

Notufnahm

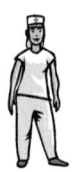

nurse

Chrankeschwöschter

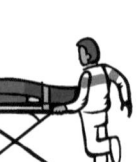

emergency

Notfall

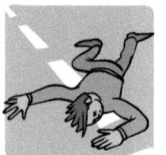

unconscious

ohnmächtig

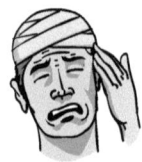

pain

Schmärz

injury

Verletzig

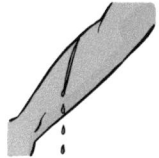

bleeding

Bluätig

heart attack

Härzinfarkt

stroke

Schlagahfall

allergy

Allergie

cough

Hueschtä

fever

Fieber

flu

Grippe

diarrhea

Durchfall

headache

Kopfschmärze

cancer

Kräbs

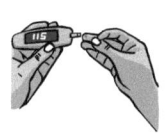

diabetes

Diabetes

surgeon

Chirurg

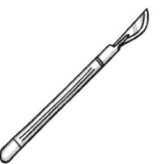

scalpel

Skalpell

operation

Operation

CT
CT

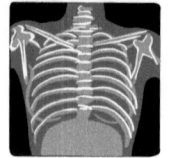

x-ray
Röntgä

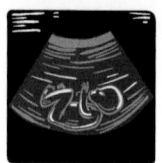

ultrasound
Ultraschall

face mask
Gsichtsmaske

disease
Krankhet

waiting room
Wartezimmer

crutch
Krückä

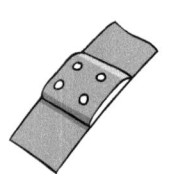

plaster
Pflaster

bandage
Vrband

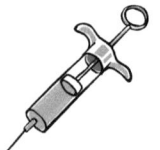

injection
Injektion

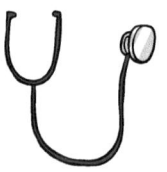

stethoscope
Stethoskop

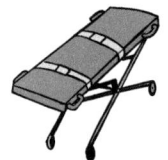

stretcher
Trage

clinical thermometer
Thermometer

birth
Geburt

overweight
Übergwicht

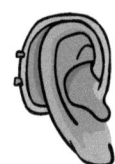

hearing aid

Hörgrät

disinfectant

Desinfektionsmittel

infection

Infektion

virus

Virus

HIV / AIDS

HIV / AIDS

medicine

Medizin

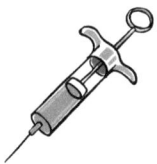

vaccination

Impfig

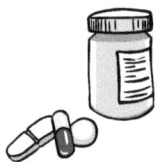

tablets

Tablette

pill

Pille

emergency call

Notruef

blood pressure monitor

Bluetdruck-Mässgrät

ill / healthy

chrank / gsund

Help!

Hiufe!

alarm

Alarm

assault

Überfall

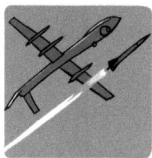

attack

Ahgriff

danger

Gfohr

emergency exit

Notuusgang

Fire!

Füür!

fire extinguisher

Füürlöscher

accident

Unfall

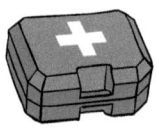

first-aid kit

Ersti-Hilf-Koffer

SOS

SOS

police

Polizei

Europe

Europa

North America

Nordamerika

South America

Südamerika

Africa

Afrika

Asia

Asie

Australia

Auschtralie

Atlantic

Atlantik

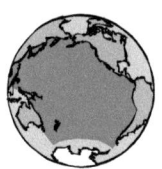

Pacific

Pazifik

Indian Ocean

Indische Ozean

Antarctic Ocean

Antarktische Ozean

Arctic Ocean

Arktische Ozean

North pole

Nordpol

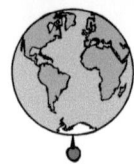

South pole

Südpol

Antarctica

Antarktis

earth

Ärde

land

Land

sea

Meer

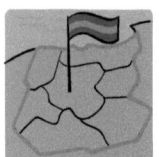

island

Inslä

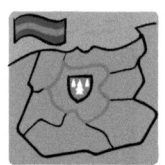

nation

Nation

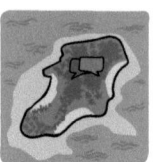

state

Staat

clock face

Ziffereblatt

hour hand

Stundezeiger

minute hand

Minutezeiger

second hand

Sekundezeiger

What time is it?

Wie spaht isch es?

day

Tag

time

Zit

now

jetzt

digital watch

Digitaluhr

minute

Minute

hour

Stunde

week
Wuche

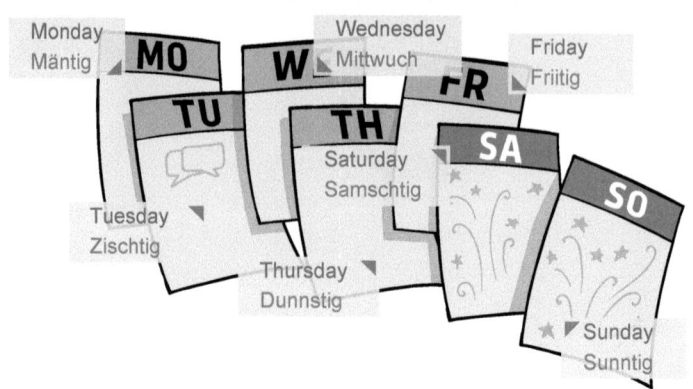

Monday / Mäntig — MO
Wednesday / Mittwuch — W
Friday / Friitig — FR
TU
TH
Tuesday / Zischtig
Saturday / Samschtig — SA
Thursday / Dunnstig
Sunday / Sunntig — SO

yesterday
geschter

today
hüt

tomorrow
morn

morning
Morgä

noon
Mittag

evening
Aabig

workdays
Wärktag

weekend
Wuchenänd

year
Johr

rain
Räge
spring
Früelig
summer
Summer
wind
Wind
fall
Herbscht
snow
Schnee
winter
Winter

4.APRIL 11°
5.APRIL 4°
6.APRIL 13°
7.APRIL 8°
8.APRIL 10°

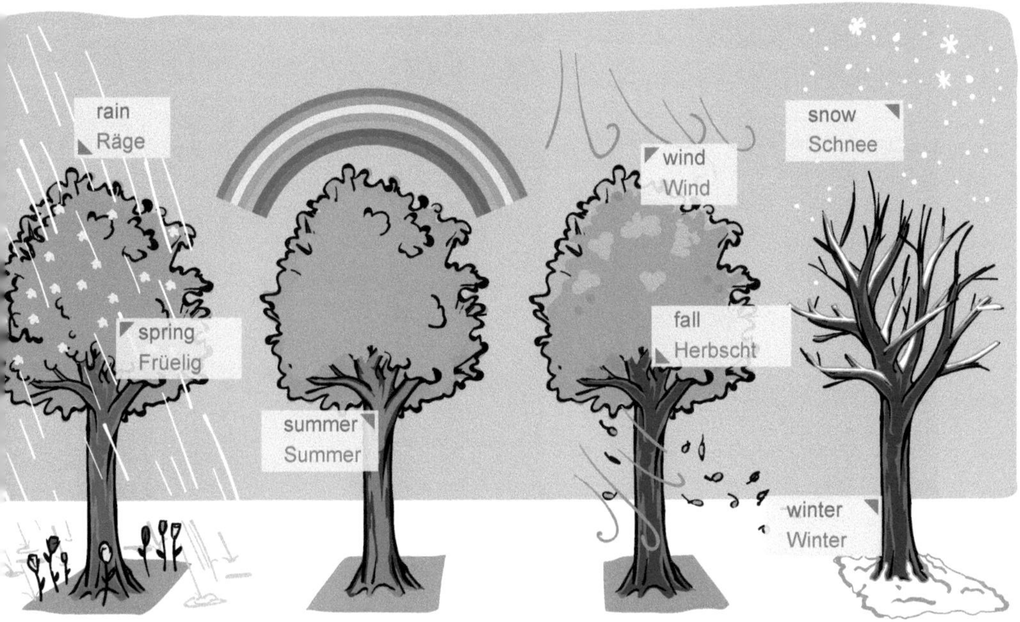

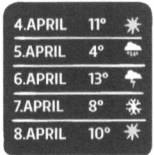

weather forecast
....
Wättervorhärsag

F C
120 40
90 30
60 20
30 10
0 0
-30 -10
-20

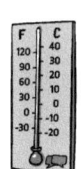

thermometer
....
Thermometer

sunshine
....
Sunneschiin

cloud
....
Wolkä

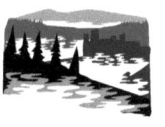

fog
....
Näbel

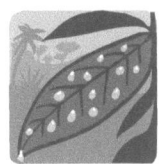

humidity
....
Fiechtigkeit

lightning

Blitz

thunder

Dunner

storm

Sturm

hail

Hagel

monsoon

Monsun

flood

Fluet

ice

Iis

January

Januar

February

Februar

March

März

April

April

May

Mai

June

Juni

July

Juli

August

Auguscht

September
Septämber

October
Oktober

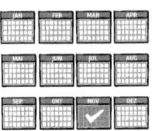

November
Novämber

December
Dezämber

shapes
Forme

circle
Kreis

square
Quadrat

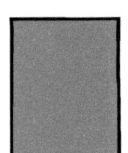

rectangle
Rächteck

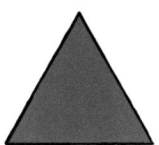

triangle
Dreieck

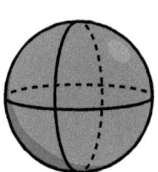

sphere
Chugele

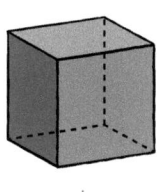

cube
Würfel

white
....
wiss

yellow
....
gäl

orange
....
orange

pink
....
pink

red
....
rot

purple
....
liila

blue
....
blau

green
....
grüen

brown
....
bruun

gray
....
grau

black
....
schwarz

a lot / a little

viel / wenig

angry / calm

hässig / ruhig

beautiful / ugly

hübsch / hässlich

beginning / end

Ahfang / Ändi

big / small

gross / chli

bright / dark

hell / dunkel

brother / sister

Brüeder / Schwöschter

clean / dirty

suuber / dräckig

complete / incomplete

vollständig / unvollständig

day / night

Tag / Nacht

dead / alive

tot / läbig

wide / narrow

breit / schmal

edible / inedible

ässbar / nid ässbar

evil / kind

bös / fründlich

excited / bored

uffreggt / glangwilt

fat / thin

dick / dünn

first / last

zerscht / zletscht

friend / enemy

Fründ / Find

full / empty

voll / läär

hard / soft

hart / weich

heavy / light

schwer / liecht

hunger / thirst

Hunger / Durscht

ill / healthy

chrank / gsund

illegal / legal

illegal / legal

intelligent / stupid

intelligänt / gatz

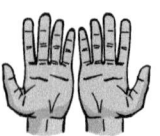

left / right

links / rächts

near / far

nöch / wiit weg

new / used
neu / bruucht

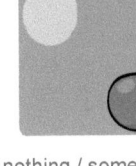

nothing / something
nüt / öpis

old / young
alt / jung

on / off
ah / uss

open / closed
offe / zue

quiet / loud
lislig / luut

rich / poor
riich / arm

right / wrong
richtig / falsch

rough / smooth
rau / glatt

sad / happy
truurig / glücklich

short / long
churz / lang

slow / fast
langsam / schnäll

wet / dry
nass / trochä

warm / cool
warm / chalt

war / peace
Chrieg / Friede

0	**1**	**2**
zero	one	two
Null	eis	zwei

3	**4**	**5**
three	four	five
drü	vier	foif

6	**7**	**8**
six	seven	eight
sächs	sibe	acht

9	**10**	**11**
nine	ten	eleven
nün	zäh	elf

12

twelve

zwölf

13

thirteen

drizäh

14

fourteen

vierzäh

15

fifteen

füfzäh

16

sixteen

sächzäh

17

seventeen

siebzäh

18

eighteen

achtzäh

19

nineteen

nünzäh

20

twenty

zwänzg

100

hundred

Hundert

1.000

thousand

Tuusig

1.000.000

million

Million

languages
Sprache

English

Änglisch

American English

Amerikanischs Änglisch

Chinese Mandarin

Chinesisch Mandarin

Hindi

Hindi

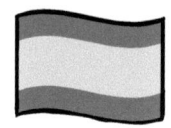

Spanish

Spanisch

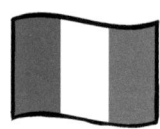

French

Französisch

Arabic

Arabisch

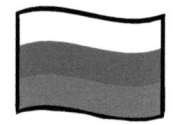

Russian

Russisch

Portuguese

Portugiesisch

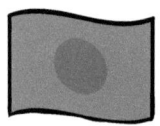

Bengali

Bengalisch

German

Dütsch

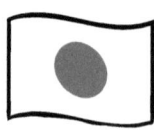

Japanese

Japanisch

I

ich

you

du

he / she / it

är / sie / es

we

mir

you

ihr

they

sie

who?

wär?

what?

was?

how?

wie?

where?

wo?

when?

wänn?

name

Name

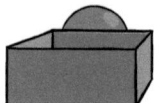

behind

hinder

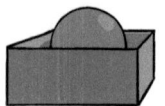

in

in

in front of

vor

over

über

on

uf

under

under

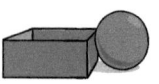

beside

näbe

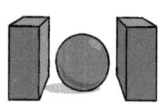

between

zwüsche

place

Ort